MW00365502

Daily Gifts

A FIVE-YEAR GRATITUDE JOURNAL

PETER PAUPER PRESS, INC.
White Plains, New York

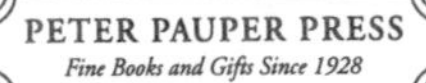

Our Company

In 1928, at the age of twenty-two, Peter Beilenson began printing books on a small press in the basement of his parents' home in Larchmont, New York. Peter—and later his wife Edna—sought to create fine books that sold at "prices even a pauper could afford."

Today, still family owned and operated, Peter Pauper Press continues to honor our founders' legacy—and our customers' expectations—of beauty, quality, and value.

Illustrations by Design Works International

Designed by Heather Zschock

Peter Pauper Press, Inc.
202 Mamaroneck Avenue
White Plains, NY 10601

ISBN 978-1-4413-0907-5
Printed in China
7 6 5 4 3 2

Visit us at www.peterpauper.com

User's Guide

We can only be said to be alive in those moments when our hearts are conscious of our treasures.

THORNTON WILDER

Sometimes in the hustle and bustle of our busy lives, we lose sight of the good things that surround us—friends, family, the beauty of trees, or a city skyline. How can we deepen our appreciation of these things? Keep a journal in which you honor the gifts in your life. Take a moment each day to count your blessings, and hold in your heart one thing that you are especially thankful for. It may be something as simple as a delicious breakfast, or a smooth morning commute to work. Or it could be the smile on a loved one's face, a sunny day, or a favorite song. Whatever it is, record one thing that you are thankful for each day in this journal, making gratitude a habit that enriches your life. You can start on any day of the year. Flip to that page and write in the appropriate year. Then continue, page by page, to fill in your daily gifts that you are thankful for. At the end of one year, flip back to your very first entry. You will have come full-circle. Then continue with the second year, below your first year's entry, and so on. By the end, you'll have a book of daily gifts to treasure and renew your sense of gratefulness.

In our daily lives, we must see that it is not happiness that makes us grateful, but the gratefulness that makes us happy.

Albert Clarke

january first

20

20

20

20

20

january second
20
20
20
20
20

january third

january fourth

20

20

20

20

20

january fifth

20

20

20

20

20

january sixth
20
20
20
20
20

january seventh

20

20

20

20

20

january eighth

20

20

20

20

20

january ninth

20

20

20

20

20

january tenth

20

20

20

20

20

january eleventh

20

20

20

20

20

january twelfth
20
20
20
20
20

january thirteenth

20

20

20

20

20

january fourteenth

20

20

20

20

20

january fifteenth

20

20

20

20

20

january sixteenth

20

20

20

20

20

january seventeenth

20

20

20

20

20

january eighteenth
20
20
20
20
20

january nineteenth

20

20

20

20

20

january twentieth
20
20
20
20
20

january twenty-first

20

20

20

20

20

january twenty-second
20
20
20
20
20

january twenty-third

20

20

20

20

20

january twenty-fourth
20
20
20
20
20

january twenty-fifth

20

20

20

20

20

january twenty-sixth

20

20

20

20

20

january twenty-seventh

20

20

20

20

20

january twenty-eighth

20

20

20

20

20

january twenty-ninth

20

20

20

20

20

january thirtieth
20
20
20
20
20

january thirty-first

20

20

20

20

20

february first

20

20

20

20

20

february second

20

20

20

20

20

february third
20
20
20
20
20

february fourth

20

20

20

20

20

february fifth
20
20
20
20
20

february sixth
20
20
20
20
20

february seventh

february eighth

february ninth

20

20

20

20

20

february tenth

20

20

20

20

20

february eleventh
20
20
20
20
20

february twelfth

20

20

20

20

20

february thirteenth
20
20
20
20
20

february fourteenth

20

20

20

20

20

february fifteenth
20
20
20
20
20

february sixteenth
20
20
20
20
20

february seventeenth
20
20
20
20
20

february eighteenth

20

20

20

20

20

february nineteenth
20
20
20
20
20

february twentieth

20

20

20

20

20

february twenty-first
20
20
20
20
20

february twenty-second

20

20

20

20

20

february twenty-third
20
20
20
20
20

february twenty-fourth

20

20

20

20

20

february twenty-fifth
20
20
20
20
20

february twenty-sixth

20

20

20

20

20

february twenty-seventh
20
20
20
20
20

february twenty-eighth
20
20
20
20
20

february twenty-ninth

march first

20

20

20

20

20

march second

march third
20
20
20
20
20

march fourth
20
20
20
20
20

march fifth

20

20

20

20

20

march sixth
20
20
20
20
20

march seventh

20

20

20

20

20

march ninth
20
20
20
20
20

march tenth
20
20
20
20
20

march eleventh
20
20
20
20
20

march twelfth
20
20
20
20
20

march thirteenth

20

20

20

20

20

march fourteenth
20
20
20
20
20

march fifteenth

20

20

20

20

20

march sixteenth
20
20
20
20
20

march seventeenth

20

20

20

20

20

march eighteenth
20
20
20
20
20

march nineteenth

20

20

20

20

20

march twentieth
20
20
20
20
20

march twenty-first

20

20

20

20

20

march twenty-second
20
20
20
20
20

march twenty-third

20

20

20

20

20

march twenty-fourth
20
20
20
20
20

march twenty-fifth

20

20

20

20

20

march twenty-sixth
20
20
20
20
20

march twenty-seventh

20

20

20

20

20

march twenty-eighth
20
20
20
20
20

march twenty-ninth

20

20

20

20

20

march thirtieth
20
20
20
20
20

march thirty-first

20

20

20

20

20

april first
20
20
20
20
20

april second
20
20
20
20
20

april third
20
20
20
20
20

april fourth
20
20
20
20
20

april fifth
20
20
20
20
20

april sixth

20

20

20

20

20

april seventh
20
20
20
20
20

april eighth
20
20
20
20
20

april ninth
20
20
20
20
20

april tenth

april eleventh
20
20
20
20
20

april twelfth

20

20

20

20

20

april thirteenth
20
20
20
20
20

april fourteenth

20

20

20

20

20

april fifteenth
20
20
20
20
20

april sixteenth

20

20

20

20

20

april seventeenth
20
20
20
20
20

april eighteenth

20

20

20

20

20

april nineteenth
20
20
20
20
20

april twentieth

20

20

20

20

20

april twenty-first
20
20
20
20
20

april twenty-second

20

20

20

20

20

april twenty-third
20
20
20
20
20

april twenty-fourth

20

20

20

20

20

april twenty-fifth
20
20
20
20
20

april twenty-sixth

20

20

20

20

20

april twenty-seventh
20
20
20
20
20

april twenty-eighth

20

20

20

20

20

april twenty-ninth
20
20
20
20
20

april thirtieth

20

20

20

20

20

may first
20
20
20
20
20

may second
20
20
20
20
20

may third
20
20
20
20
20

may fourth
20
20
20
20
20

may fifth

20

20

20

20

20

may sixth
20
20
20
20
20

may seventh
20
20
20
20
20

may eighth
20
20
20
20
20

may ninth
20
20
20
20
20

may tenth
20
20
20
20
20

may eleventh
20
20
20
20
20

may twelfth
20
20
20
20
20

may thirteenth

20

20

20

20

20

may fourteenth

20

20

20

20

20

may fifteenth
20
20
20
20
20

may sixteenth

20

20

20

20

20

may seventeenth
20
20
20
20
20

may eighteenth

20

20

20

20

20

may nineteenth
20
20
20
20
20

may twentieth

20

20

20

20

20

may twenty-first
20
20
20
20
20

may twenty-second

20

20

20

20

20

may twenty-third
20
20
20
20
20

may twenty-fourth

20

20

20

20

20

may twenty-fifth
20
20
20
20
20

may twenty-sixth

20

20

20

20

20

may twenty-seventh
20
20
20
20
20

may twenty-eighth

20

20

20

20

20

may twenty-ninth
20
20
20
20
20

may thirtieth
20
20
20
20
20

may thirty-first
20
20
20
20
20

june first

20

20

20

20

20

june second
20
20
20
20
20

june third
20
20
20
20
20

june fourth
20
20
20
20
20

june fifth
20
20
20
20
20

june sixth
20
20
20
20
20

june seventh
20
20
20
20
20

june eighth
20
20
20
20
20

june ninth

20

20

20

20

20

june tenth
20
20
20
20
20

june eleventh
20
20
20
20
20

june twelfth
20
20
20
20
20

june thirteenth

20

20

20

20

20

june fourteenth
20
20
20
20
20

june fifteenth
20
20
20
20
20

june sixteenth

20

20

20

20

20

june seventeenth

20

20

20

20

20

june eighteenth
20
20
20
20
20

june nineteenth

20

20

20

20

20

june twentieth

20

20

20

20

20

june twenty-first

20

20

20

20

20

june twenty-second
20
20
20
20
20

june twenty-third

20

20

20

20

20

20

20

20

20

20

june twenty-fifth

20

20

20

20

20

june twenty-sixth

20

20

20

20

20

june twenty-seventh
20
20
20
20
20

june twenty-eighth
20
20
20
20
20

june twenty-ninth

20

20

20

20

20

june thirtieth
20
20
20
20
20

july first

july second
20
20
20
20
20

july third

20

20

20

20

20

july fourth
20
20
20
20
20

july fifth

20

20

20

20

20

july sixth
20
20
20
20
20

july seventh
20
20
20
20
20

july eighth
20
20
20
20
20

july ninth

20

20

20

20

20

july tenth
20
20
20
20
20

july eleventh
20
20
20
20
20

july twelfth
20
20
20
20
20

july thirteenth
20
20
20
20
20

july fourteenth
20
20
20
20
20

july fifteenth

20

20

20

20

20

july sixteenth

20

20

20

20

20

july seventeenth
20
20
20
20
20

july eighteenth
20
20
20
20
20

july nineteenth

20

20

20

20

20

july twentieth
20
20
20
20
20

july twenty-first

20

20

20

20

20

july twenty-second

20

20

20

20

20

july twenty-third

20

20

20

20

20

july twenty-fourth
20
20
20
20
20

july twenty-fifth

20

20

20

20

20

july twenty-sixth
20
20
20
20
20

july twenty-seventh

20

20

20

20

20

july twenty-eighth

20

20

20

20

20

july twenty-ninth

20

20

20

20

20

july thirtieth
20
20
20
20
20

july thirty-first
20
20
20
20
20

august first
20
20
20
20
20

august second

20

20

20

20

20

august third
20
20
20
20
20

august fourth

august fifth
20
20
20
20
20

august sixth

20

20

20

20

20

august seventh
20
20
20
20
20

august eighth

20

20

20

20

20

august ninth
20
20
20
20
20

20

20

20

20

20

august eleventh
20
20
20
20
20

august twelfth
20
20
20
20
20

august thirteenth
20
20
20
20
20

august fourteenth

20

20

20

20

20

august fifteenth
20
20
20
20
20

august sixteenth

august seventeenth
20
20
20
20
20

august eighteenth

20

20

20

20

20

august nineteenth

20

20

20

20

20

august twentieth

20

20

20

20

20

august twenty-first
20
20
20
20
20

august twenty-second

20

20

20

20

20

august twenty-third
20
20
20
20
20

august twenty-fourth

20

20

20

20

20

august twenty-fifth

20

20

20

20

20

august twenty-sixth
20
20
20
20
20

august twenty-seventh
20
20
20
20
20

august twenty-eighth

20

20

20

20

20

august twenty-ninth
20
20
20
20
20

august thirtieth

20

20

20

20

20

august thirty-first
20
20
20
20
20

september first

20

20

20

20

20

september second
20
20
20
20
20

september third

20

20

20

20

20

september fourth
20
20
20
20
20

september fifth

20

20

20

20

20

september sixth
20
20
20
20
20

september seventh

september eighth
20
20
20
20
20

september ninth

20

20

20

20

20

september tenth
20
20
20
20
20

september eleventh

september twelfth
20
20
20
20
20

september thirteenth

20

20

20

20

20

september fourteenth

20

20

20

20

20

september fifteenth

20

20

20

20

20

20
20
20
20
20

september seventeenth
20
20
20
20
20

september eighteenth

september nineteenth

20

20

20

20

20

september twentieth
20
20
20
20
20

september twenty-first

20

20

20

20

20

september twenty-second
20
20
20
20
20

september twenty-third

20

20

20

20

20

september twenty-fourth
20
20
20
20
20

september twenty-fifth

20

20

20

20

20

september twenty-sixth
20
20
20
20
20

september twenty-seventh

20

20

20

20

20

september twenty-eighth
20
20
20
20
20

september twenty-ninth

20

20

20

20

20

september thirtieth
20
20
20
20
20

october first

20

20

20

20

20

october second
20
20
20
20
20

october third
20
20
20
20
20

october fourth
20
20
20
20
20

october fifth
20
20
20
20
20

october sixth
20
20
20
20
20

october seventh

20

20

20

20

20

october eighth
20
20
20
20
20

october ninth

20

20

20

20

20

october tenth
20
20
20
20
20

october eleventh

20

20

20

20

20

october twelfth
20
20
20
20
20

october thirteenth

october fourteenth
20
20
20
20
20

october fifteenth

20

20

20

20

20

october sixteenth
20
20
20
20
20

october seventeenth

20

20

20

20

20

october eighteenth

20

20

20

20

20

october nineteenth

20

20

20

20

20

october twentieth
20
20
20
20
20

october twenty-first

20

20

20

20

20

october twenty-second
20
20
20
20
20

october twenty-third

20

20

20

20

20

october twenty-fourth
20
20
20
20
20

october twenty-fifth

20

20

20

20

20

october twenty-sixth
20
20
20
20
20

october twenty-seventh

20

20

20

20

20

october twenty-eighth
20
20
20
20
20

october twenty-ninth

20

20

20

20

20

october thirtieth
20
20
20
20
20

october thirty-first

20

20

20

20

20

november first
20
20
20
20
20

november second

20

20

20

20

20

november third
20
20
20
20
20

november fourth

20

20

20

20

20

november fifth
20
20
20
20
20

november sixth

20

20

20

20

20

november seventh
20
20
20
20
20

november eighth

20

20

20

20

20

november ninth
20
20
20
20
20

november tenth

20

20

20

20

20

november eleventh
20
20
20
20
20

november twelfth

20

20

20

20

20

november thirteenth
20
20
20
20
20

november fourteenth

20

20

20

20

20

november fifteenth
20
20
20
20
20

november sixteenth

20

20

20

20

20

november seventeenth
20
20
20
20
20

november eighteenth

20

20

20

20

20

november nineteenth
20
20
20
20
20

november twentieth

20

20

20

20

20

november twenty-first

20

20

20

20

20

november twenty-second

20

20

20

20

20

november twenty-third
20
20
20
20
20

november twenty-fourth

20

20

20

20

20

november twenty-fifth
20
20
20
20
20

november twenty-sixth

20

20

20

20

20

november twenty-seventh
20
20
20
20
20

november twenty-eighth

20

20

20

20

20

november twenty-ninth
20
20
20
20
20

november thirtieth

20

20

20

20

20

december first

20

20

20

20

20

december second

20

20

20

20

20

december third
20
20
20
20
20

december fourth
20
20
20
20
20

december fifth
20
20
20
20
20

december sixth
20
20
20
20
20

december seventh
20
20
20
20
20

december eighth
20
20
20
20
20

december ninth

20

20

20

20

20

december tenth

20

20

20

20

20

december eleventh
20
20
20
20
20

december twelfth

december thirteenth
20
20
20
20
20

december fourteenth

20

20

20

20

20

december fifteenth
20
20
20
20
20

december sixteenth

20

20

20

20

20

december seventeenth
20
20
20
20
20

december eighteenth

20

20

20

20

20

december nineteenth
20
20
20
20
20

december twentieth

20

20

20

20

20

december twenty-first

20

20

20

20

20

december twenty-second

20

20

20

20

20

december twenty-third

20

20

20

20

20

december twenty-fourth

20

20

20

20

20

december twenty-fifth

20

20

20

20

20

december twenty-sixth

20

20

20

20

20

december twenty-seventh

20

20

20

20

20

december twenty-eighth

20

20

20

20

20

december twenty-ninth
20
20
20
20
20

december thirtieth

december thirty-first

20

20

20

20

20

notes

notes